NEXT GENERATION ACCUPLACER

READING PRACTICE TESTS

WITH EXAM TIPS

Next Generation Accuplacer Reading Practice Tests with Exam Tips

ISBN-13: 978-1-949282-28-3

ISBN-10: 1-949282-28-7

Accuplacer and Accuplacer Next Generation are registered trademarks of the College Board, which is neither affiliated with nor endorses this publication.

TABLE OF CONTENTS

Accuplacer Reading Practice Test 1

Accuplacer Reading Practice Test 1

Read the passages and answers the questions based on what is stated or implied in the text.

Working in a run-down laboratory near Paris, Marie Curie worked around the clock to discover a radioactive element. When she finally captured her quarry, she named it "radium" after the Latin word meaning ray. She had spent the day blending chemical compounds which could be used to destroy unhealthy cells in the body. As she was about to retire to bed that evening, she decided to return to her lab. There she found that the chemical compound had become crystalized in the bowls and was emitting the elusive light that she sought.

Inspired by the French scientist Henri Becquerel, Curie won the Nobel Prize for Chemistry for her discovery. Upon winning the prize, she declared that the radioactive element would be used only to treat disease and would not be used for commercial profit. Today radium provides an effective remedy for certain types of cancer. Radium, now used for a treatment called radiotherapy, works by inundating diseased cells with radioactive particles. Its success lies in the fact that it eradicates malignant cells without any lasting ill effects on the body.

1. Which of the following best describes the organization of the passage?
    A. A lingering doubt is clarified, and then a further question is posed.
    B. The background to a discovery is discussed, and then the reasons for its current use are explained.
    C. A problem is presented, and then a solution is proposed.
    D. Historical information is provided, and then a unique scenario is presented to illustrate the information.

Tip: For questions on the organization or structure of the passage, find the main idea of each paragraph and compare these to the answer choices.

Two original forms of theater have emerged from Japanese culture: Noh and Kabuki. Noh, the older form, was originally established to meet the demands of the "discriminating Japanese aristocracy" and remained "unchanged for more than six centuries." Noh renders mundane, everyday activities, like drinking tea or arranging flowers, into exquisite artistic performances. Consisting of minimal spectacle, bare stage designs, and little spoken dialogue, Noh is classified as more ritual than drama. In order to convey the dialogue, a chorus sings the protagonist's lines while the performer engages in the "solemn act" of the dance.

Kabuki performances are discernably different than those of Noh. Based on puppet theater, Kabuki is designed to meet the tastes of the general populace, rather than those of the aristocracy. Because of its appeal to the general populace, Kabuki theater remains as fascinating and exotic as it has always been, even though its purity has been somewhat compromised through exposure to other cultures.

2. The use of quoted material in the passage suggests which of the following about followers of Noh?

   A. They lament the fact that Noh clings on to outdated customs of the past.

   B. They believe that Kabuki theater is overtly flamboyant.

   C. They fear that the popularity of Kabuki theater may diminish the appeal of Noh.

   D. The followers of Noh are traditional, discerning, and serious.

Tip: Questions that ask you about the use of quotation marks or capital letters are often really inference questions. Think about synonyms for the words in the quotation marks to help choose the answer.

How is civil order maintained within any given population? The civil order control function suggests that public order is best maintained through agencies other than the police force or militia. Martial law, the establishment of military rule over a civilian population, is only imposed when other methods of civil control have proven ineffective. In the past, this state of affairs most commonly occurred to quell uprisings during periods of colonial occupation or quash sectarian groups.

So, how is the declaration of martial law currently regulated? The constitutions of many countries now make provisions for the introduction of martial law, allowing it only in cases of national emergency or in the case of threats to national security from foreign countries. In democratic nations, severe restrictions are imposed on the implementation of martial law, meaning that a formal declaration of military rule over a nation should be rendered virtually impractical.

3.   Which of the following statements best explains the differences between how martial law was instituted in the past and how it is instituted at present?

    A. In the past, the militia was not used to support civil authorities, although it is used this way at present.

    B. In the past, countries did not have constitutions or other established means to regulate the declaration of martial law.

    C. There are more threats to national security nowadays than there were in the past.

    D. Civil order was more difficult to maintain in the past than it is during the present time.

Tip: For questions on understanding relationships among past and present events in a passage, look for linking words that indicate a change in the time period. Examples: At present, Now, Currently

The pyramids at Giza in Egypt are still among the world's largest structures, even today. The monuments were constructed well before the wheel was invented, and it is notable that the Egyptians had only the most primitive, handmade tools to complete the massive project. Copper saws were used to cut softer stones, as well as the large wooden posts that levered the stone blocks into their final places. Wooden mallets were used to drive flint wedges into rocks in order to split them. The Egyptians also utilized drills that were fashioned from wood and twine. In order to ensure that the stones were level, wooden rods were joined by strips of twine to check that the surfaces of the stone blocks were flat. Finally, the stone blocks were put onto wooden rockers so that they could more easily be placed into their correct positions on the pyramid.

4. What is the writer's main purpose?

A. to give a step-by-step explanation of the construction of the Giza pyramids

B. to compare the construction of the Giza pyramids to that of modern day structures

C. to give an overview of some of the main implements that were used to construct the Giza pyramids

D. to highlight the importance of the achievement of the construction of the Giza pyramids

Tip: The main purpose of a passage will usually be to describe something or to persuade the reader about a particular point of view. The above passage is descriptive, so determine what the writer's primarily focus is. For persuasion passages, you need to look for adjectives or phrases that convey the writer's point of view.

The Earth's only natural satellite, the moon lacks its own atmosphere and is only about one-fourth the size of the planet it orbits. The equality of its orbital rate to that of the Earth is the result of gravitational locking, also known as synchronous rotation. Thus, the same hemisphere of the Moon always faces the earth. The brightest lunar surface areas are formed from meteoric material, while its dark surface regions, called mare basalts or basaltic plains, are the result of volcanic flooding related to impacts from asteroids. Scientific dating of samples from the Moon's crust reveals that the materials range in age from three to four billion years old.

Lunar evolution models suggest that the development of the Moon occurred in five principle stages. Because of the geological and mineral composition of the surface of the Moon, one popular theory hypothesizes that the Moon grew out of debris that was dislodged from the Earth's crust following the impact of a large object with the planet.

5.   For which of the following situations does the concept of synchronous rotation, as it is defined in the passage, provide the most likely explanation?

A. The Moon goes through four phases every twenty-eight days.

B. Two objects fall to the ground at the same speed and land at the same time.

C. Stars appear to shine at the same intensity, regardless of their position in the sky.

D. A telecommunications satellite always appears in the same position above a certain city on Earth.

Tip: For questions that ask you to read closely to determine a specific concept, you need to focus on a specific detail in the passage. In this passage, we are focusing on the concept of synchronous rotation, which explains why the same hemisphere of the Moon always faces the earth.

Questions 6 to 9 refer to the following passage.

One of those sprawling flamboyant patterns committing every artistic sin. It is dull enough to confuse the eye in following, pronounced enough to constantly irritate and provoke study, and when you follow the lame uncertain curves for a little distance they suddenly commit suicide—plunge off at outrageous angles, destroy themselves in unheard of contradictions.

The color is repellent, almost revolting; a smoldering unclean yellow, strangely faded by the slow-turning sunlight. It is a dull yet lurid orange in some places, a sickly sulfur tint in others. No wonder the children hated it! I should hate it myself if I had to live in this room long.

These nervous troubles are dreadfully depressing. John does not know how much I really suffer. He knows there is no REASON to suffer, and that satisfies him. Of course it is only nervousness. It does weigh on me so not to do my duty in any way!

I meant to be such a help to John, such a real rest and comfort, and here I am a comparative burden already!

Nobody would believe what an effort it is to do what little I am able—to dress and entertain, and other things. It is fortunate Mary is so good with the baby. Such a dear baby! And yet I cannot be with him, it makes me so nervous.

I suppose John never was nervous in his life. He laughs at me so about this wall-paper! At first he meant to repaper the room, but afterwards he said that I was letting it get the better of me, and that nothing was worse for a nervous patient than to give way to such fancies. He said that after the wall-paper was changed it would be the heavy bedstead, and then the barred windows, and then that gate at the head of the stairs, and so on.

"You know the place is doing you good," he said, "and really, dear, I don't care to renovate the house just for a three months' rental."

I wish I could get well faster. But I must not think about that. This paper looks to me as if it knew what a vicious influence it had! (Excerpt from *The Yellow Wallpaper* by Charlotte Perkins Gilman)

6. When the narrator uses the word "it" in paragraph 1, she is referring to:

    A. the room.

    B. the baby.

    C. the wallpaper.

    D. the heavy bedstead.

Tip: For questions on analyzing word choice rhetorically, you need to look for synonyms for the word in question. Notice that after using the word "it" in paragraph 1, the writer describes the pattern and color of the object. Continue reading to discover what the object is later in the passage.

7. The use of capitalization in paragraph 3 is intended to reinforce which of the following thoughts from the point of view of the narrator?

    A. She wants to imply that her husband thinks that she is irrational.

    B. She is trying to point out the gravity of her situation.

    C. She wants to suggest that men are more reasonable than women.

    D. She is praising her husband for being logical.

8. The tone of the passage implies that the relationship between the narrator and her husband is:

   A. contented.

   B. strained.

   C. resigned.

   D. violent.

9. From this passage, we can infer that the narrator:

   A. is a poor mother.

   B. regrets her marriage.

   C. is not in good mental health.

   D. could be dangerous to society.

Questions 10 to 13 refer to the following pair of passages.

Passage 1:

Credit card debt is a major cause of over one million bankruptcies each year. The reason is that many people get a credit card on impulse and fail to read the terms and conditions. By the time annual fees are accrued, payments can be missed, which causes balances to skyrocket.

Although we all would like to believe that credit card companies are culpable, individuals themselves are the real culprits. In short, if your credit card debt is out of control, the real cause of your financial mess is you. If you can summon enough willpower and strength to manage your finances and spending, then you will find yourself the winner in the game of finance. It may be easy to get into debt, but getting out of debt is much more difficult. One simple phrase sums up the solution to financial problems: If you don't have the money to spend, then don't spend it.

Passage 2:

It has to be said that external forces and market conditions have a huge impact on personal financial situations. Have you ever noticed that the things you buy at the store go up a few pennies between shopping trips? Not every week and not by much – just little by little – but they continue to creep up. There is a way that the effect of price increases upon personal finances can be minimized: buy in quantity when prices are low. My philosophy is to set out to find the best prices I can get on quantity purchases of things such as bathroom items and dry and canned food, even if I have to increase my credit card debt to get them. You will be surprised by how much you can save, for example, by buying a twenty pound bag of rice as opposed to a one pound bag.

10.   Which best describes the relationship between Passage 1 and Passage 2?

   A. Passage 1 introduces a theory that is discussed at length in Passage 2.

   B. Passage 1 recounts a personal experience that is supported by Passage 2.

   C. Passage 1 reveals a particular opinion on a topic, while Passage 2 provides an alternative point of view.

   D. Passage 2 refutes the scientific evidence that is provided in Passage 1.

Tip: For questions on understanding relationships between paired passages, you will need to determine if the passages are descriptive or persuasive. These paired passages are persuasive, so we need to look for and then compare the writer's point of view in each passage.

11.   The reference to "credit card debt" in passage 1 serves to:

   A. defer to authority.

   B. provide a contrast.

   C. offer an explanation.

   D. reveal a cause.

12. The writer of passage 1 would disagree most strongly with which of the following assertions from passage 2?

    A. External forces and market conditions have a huge impact on personal financial situations.

    B. The things you buy at the store go up a few pennies between shopping trips.

    C. There is a way that the effect of price increases upon personal finances can be minimized: buy in quantity when prices are low.

    D. My philosophy is to set out to find the best prices I can get on quantity purchases of things such as bathroom items and dry and canned food, even if I have to increase my credit card debt to get them.

13.   Which of the following words best characterizes how both authors view

avoiding unnecessary expenses?

A. advantageous

B. undisciplined

C. victorious

D. philosophical

Tip: This is a question on comparing passages for specific concepts. In these

paired passages, we are looking for the specific concept of avoiding unnecessary

expenses. This specific concept is summed up in the last sentence of each

passage. Compare these sentences to find the answer.

---

(1) The world's first public railway carried passengers, even though it was primarily designed to transport coal from inland mines to ports on the North Sea. (2) Having thirty-two open wagons and the capacity to carry over three hundred passengers, the train was extremely popular for many significant reasons. (3) It had rimmed wheels which ran atop rails that were specially designed to give the carriages a faster and smoother ride. (4) While the small carriages could hardly be termed commodious, the locomotive could accelerate to 15 miles per hour, a record-breaking speed at that time. (5) Later, the inventor of the locomotive, George Stephenson, revolutionized his steam engine by adding twenty-four further pipes. (6) Now containing twenty-five tubes instead of one, Stephenson's second "iron horse" was even faster and more powerful than his first creation.

14. Which of the following does the writer offer as evidence to support his claim in Sentence 2 that "the train was extremely popular for many significant reasons"?

A. The fact that this was the first train of this type.

B. The mention of the speed and relative comfort of the train.

C. The fact that the train was design to transport coal.

D. The description of Stevenson's other inventions.

Tip: When answering questions on the analysis of evidence in support of claims, carefully analyze the sentence following the claim. So, read Sentence 3 carefully to find the support. You may then need to find synonyms in the answer choices for the key words in the supporting sentence.

Although the foundations of the movement can be traced back to the artists van Gogh and Gauguin in the late nineteenth century, the first recorded use of the term Expressionism was in Germany in the early twentieth century. Influencing art, literature, theater, and architecture, Expressionism strives to illustrate the inner emotional reaction to a reality. In this approach, the traditional notion of realism is to be disregarded, as are the conventional ideas of beauty and proportion. Accordingly, Expressionist artists use distortion, incongruous color schemes, and exaggerated shapes and sizes to reveal their emotions. The impact of the movement is also present in fictional and poetic works of the era, particularly those which represent the dislocation of the individual within society.

15. The passage suggests that Expressionism demonstrated which one of the following phenomena?

A. Artistic movements are ever-changing with the passage of time.

B. Abstract art is more popular than realistic art.

C. Human beings felt out of sync with their communities at the time this movement was taking place.

D. Most twentieth century artists were nonconventional.

Tip: This is a question on reading closely to identify explicit ideas. The question is asking us about the phenomenon that Expressionism demonstrates. The passage states: "Expressionism strives to illustrate the inner emotional reaction to a reality." What particular emotion did individuals in society feel during this time?

Known as the Centennial State, Colorado is divided into sixty-three counties. The eastern part of the state was gained by the United States in 1803 as part of the Louisiana Purchase, while the western part was acquired from Mexico by treaty in 1848. Colorado joined the union as the 38th state in 1876, shortly after the first discovery of a substantial amount of gold in the state near Pikes Peak in 1859. Agriculture in the state involves the production of an abundance of wheat, hay, corn, sugar beets, and other crops. Farmers in the state also engage in cattle ranching and raising other livestock.

16. In the passage, the use of the words "substantial," "abundance," and "engage in" serve mainly to emphasize the:

   A. writer's intention to depict Colorado as a productive state.

   B. writer's frustration that Colorado could not be more diverse.

   C. history of the founding of the state.

   D. ways in which farming operations change over time.

Tip: For questions that ask you to analyze the emphasis in the author's word choice, look at the key words in the question. Then examine the passage to see what the key words are describing.

Today archeologists are still endeavoring to uncover the secrets of Africa's past. Evidence of the earliest human activity has been found in the south and east of the continent, where climatic conditions helped to preserve the human skeletons and stone tools found there. Genetic science confirms that these are quite likely the oldest remains in the world of modern people, with this classification based on the ability of humans to become adaptable and ready to respond to environmental change. Even though the artifacts and skeletons of early Africans are most commonly found in a highly fragmented state, these findings are more than sufficient in order to make a number of significant conclusions. Perhaps the most important discovery is that there is great variation among the human remains, indicating a wide array of physical differences among members of the population. It has also been well established that the earliest species of hominids spread from Africa to other continents.

17. When the author writes that "genetic science confirms that these are quite likely the oldest remains in the world of modern people," she most likely intends to:

   A. emphasize the depth and breadth of Africa's history.

   B. explain the way that climatic conditions can help to preserve skeletons.

   C. describe the importance of the stone tools found in African sites.

   D. highlight the significance of archeological discoveries in Africa.

Tip: In order to understand the writer's intention for a specific statement, look to find similar or supporting statements within the passage. Notice that the writer also states that "these findings are more than sufficient in order to make a number of significant conclusions."

A much-loved classic of children's literature, *Alice in Wonderland* portrays a magical world inhabited by the Mad Hatter, the Cheshire Cat, the White Rabbit, the Dormouse, and the Queen of Hearts. Based on the nursery tales that the author Lewis Carroll told to the daughter of one of his academic colleagues, the story is one part of a series that was entitled *Alice's Adventures*. The sequels, *Through the Looking Glass* and *What Alice Did Next* were extremely popular at the time they were written as well. The author, whose real name was Charles Dodson, was also a gifted mathematician and enthusiastic amateur photographer.

18.   Which of the following provides the best summary of the above passage?

   A. The text describes Lewis Carrol's *Alice's Adventures* series and points out lesser-known facts about the author.

   B. The text describes general rules about Lewis Carrol's writing and states an exception to this general rule.

   C. The text describes Lewis Carrol's writing and casts doubt on a previous assertion about it.

   D. The text describes Lewis Carrol's writing and dispels a commonly-held falsehood about it.

Tip: For questions that ask you to summarize a passage, look for words and phrases such as "in addition" or "also," which signal that another idea is being added to the main idea.

19. Given the college's strict policy on academic integrity, I don't see how he

got _____ cheating on the final exam last semester.

    A. free from

    B. away with

    C. worthy of

    D. caught up

20. The articles of incorporation for any business usually require a group

_____ before any proposed course of action can be approved.

    A. consensus

    B. sinecure

    C. inauguration

    D. animosity

Tip: You will usually see two gap-fill type questions on the reading exam, which may cover vocabulary or word use.

Accuplacer Reading Practice Test 1 – Answers

1. B

2. D

3. B

4. C

5. D

6. C

7. A

8. B

9. C

10. C

11. D

12. D

13. A

14. B

15. C

16. A

17. D

18. A

19. B

20. A

Accuplacer Reading Practice Test 1 – Answers and Explanations

1.   The correct answer is B. The background to a discovery is discussed in paragraph 1, and the reasons for its current use are explained in paragraph 2. Paragraph one describes the scientist's work history and professional background. Paragraph 2 describes how the discovery is used today.

2.   The correct answer is D. The use of quotation marks in the passage suggests that followers of Noh are traditional, discerning, and serious. Paragraph 1 uses quotation marks when it states that Noh is for the "discriminating Japanese aristocracy" and that it depicts a "solemn act." The word "aristocracy" implies that the dance is traditional in nature. "Discriminating" means "discerning," and "solemn" means "serious."

3.   The correct answer is B. In the past, countries did not have constitutions or other established means to regulate the declaration of martial law. The second paragraph explains that "the constitutions of many countries now make provisions for the introduction of martial law." The use of the word "now" suggests that these provisions were not in place in the past.

4.   The correct answer is C. The writer's main purpose is to give an overview of some of the main implements that were used to construct the Giza pyramids. The passage is devoted to describing the tools that were used during the project.

5.   The correct answer is D. The concept of synchronous rotation, as it is defined in the passage, provides the most likely explanation for the situation in which

a telecommunications satellite always appears in the same position above a certain city on Earth. This is similar to the way in which the same hemisphere of the Moon always faces the earth.

6. The correct answer is C. We know that the narrator is talking about the wallpaper because she is describing the patterns on the paper. She then goes on to talk about the wallpaper in the majority of the passage.

7. The correct answer is A. For emphasis questions like this one, think about how the statement would sound if spoken aloud. The word "reason" would be emphasized if the narrator was speaking in a sarcastic way. The narrator also mentions that the conclusion that she is not being reasonable satisfies her husband. She is talking about the situation from his point of view, not hers, so she is implying that he thinks she is irrational.

8. The correct answer is B. The passage mentions various ways in which the narrator's husband will not accommodate her wishes, so the reader can assume that their relationship is difficult or strained.

9. The correct answer is C. The narrator speaks about nervousness, which is a euphemism for nervous breakdown or depression. She states at the beginning of paragraph 3: "These nervous troubles are dreadfully depressing."

10. The correct answer is C. Passage 1 reveals a particular opinion on a topic, while passage 2 provides an alternative point of view. Passage 1 is against

credit card debt, but passage 2 states that it is acceptable to increase credit card debt in certain circumstances.

11. The correct answer is D. The reference to "credit card debt" in passage 1 serves to reveal a cause. Passage 1 states: "Credit card debt is a major cause of over one million bankruptcies each year."

12. The correct answer is D. The writer of passage 1 would disagree most strongly with this statement because it directly supports increasing credit card debt.

13. The correct answer is A. Both authors view avoiding unnecessary expenses as advantageous. The writer of passage 1 supports avoiding unnecessary expenses by controlling spending. The writer of passage 2 states that unnecessary spending can be avoided by making purchases when prices are low.

14. The correct answer is B. In the next sentence, the writer mentions that the train was "designed to give the carriages a faster and smoother ride." So, we can conclude that the speed and relative comfort of the train made it popular.

15. The correct answer is C. The passage suggests that Expressionism illustrates the way in which human beings felt out of sync with their communities at the time this movement was taking place. The last sentence of the passage comments that Expressionism represents "the dislocation of the individual within society."

16. The correct answer is A. We know that it is the writer's intention to depict Colorado as a productive state because he begins the sentence as follows: "Agriculture in the state involves the production of [. . .]"

17. The correct answer is D. The author states that "genetic science confirms that these are quite likely the oldest remains in the world of modern people" in paragraph 1 primarily in order to emphasize the significance of archeological discoveries in Africa. We know this because the paragraph goes on to explain that "these findings are more than sufficient in order to make a number of significant conclusions."

18. The correct answer is A. The final sentence of the passage is as follows: "The author, whose real name was Charles Dodson, was also a gifted mathematician and enthusiastic amateur photographer." The author includes the final sentence of the passage in order to point out lesser-known facts about the subject. Many people will know that Lewis Carroll is the author of *Alice in Wonderland*. However, they may not know Lewis Carroll's real name or his other skills.

19. The correct answer is B. "Get away with" means to escape from blame.

20. The correct answer is A. "Group consensus" means that the group is in agreement about a decision or course of action.

Accuplacer Reading Practice Test 2

Questions 1 to 4 refer to the following passage.

The excellent Mr. Morris was an Englishman, and he lived in the days of Queen Victoria the Good. He was a prosperous and very sensible man; he read the Times and went to church, and as he grew towards middle age an expression of quiet contented contempt for all who were not as himself settled. Everything that it was right and proper for a man in his position to possess, he possessed.

And among other right and proper possessions, this Mr. Morris had a wife and children. They were the right sort of wife, and the right sort and number of children, of course; nothing imaginative or highty-flighty about any of them, so far as Mr. Morris could see; they wore perfectly correct clothing, neither smart nor hygienic nor faddy in any way; and they lived in a nice sensible house.

And when it was a fit and proper thing for him to do so, Mr. Morris died. His tomb was of marble, and, without any art nonsense or laudatory inscription, quietly imposing—such being the fashion of his time.

He underwent various changes according to the accepted custom in these cases, and long before this story begins his bones even had become dust, and were scattered to the four quarters of heaven. And his sons and his grandsons and his great-grandsons and his great-great-grandsons, they too were dust and ashes, and were scattered likewise. It was a thing he could not have imagined, that a day would come when even his great-great-grandsons would be scattered to the four winds of heaven. If anyone had suggested it to him he would have resented it. He was one of those worthy people who take no interest in the future of mankind at all. He had grave doubts, indeed, if there was any future for mankind after he was dead. It seemed quite impossible and quite uninteresting to imagine anything happening after he was dead. Yet the thing was so, and when even his great-great-grandson was dead and decayed and forgotten, when the sham half-timbered house had gone the way of all shams, and all that Mr. Morris had found real and important was sere and dead, the world was still going on, and people were still going about it, just as heedless and impatient of the Future, or, indeed, of anything but their own selves and property, as Mr. Morris had been. (Excerpt from *A Story of the Days to Come* by HG Wells)

1. What does the narrator imply when he states "And among other right and proper possessions, this Mr. Morris had a wife and children"?

   A. Mr. Morris felt affection toward his wife and children, although he sometimes treated them coldly.

   B. Mr. Morris got married and had a family because social convention dictated that he do so.

   C. Mr. Morris quietly resented his wife and family because they made him acquire possessions that he did not want.

   D. Mr. Morris's family awaited his passing because it meant they would come into a good inheritance.

2. What is the best meaning of "highty-flighty" as it is used in paragraph 2?

   A. empty-headed

   B. erudite

   C. sensitive

   D. unfriendly

3. The description of Mr. Morris's home and his tomb are similar because:

    A. they demonstrated no real interest in the future of mankind.

    B. they displayed the underlying resentment that Mr. Morris felt about his life.

    C. they would have been considered right and proper for the society of their time.

    D. they both reveal the heed and care that society takes about the future.

4. From the information in the above excerpt, the reader could assume that the remainder of the story is going to be about:

    A. how life in the future is different than life in the past.

    B. the narrator's regrets with his grandchildren.

    C. the protagonist's home and other possessions.

    D. spiritual aspects of the afterlife.

In his book *Il Milione*, known in English as *The Travels of Marco Polo*, the intrepid explorer describes the marvels he encountered as he journeyed to China. Upon his visit to the emperor Kublai Khan in Cathay, Polo witnessed the magical illusions performed by the court wizards of the supreme ruler. Watching in amazement as the wizards recited incantations, Polo first saw a row of golden cups levitate over the table as Khan drank from each one without spilling a drop. Polo also recounted that Khan had astonishing powers over wild animals. Unrestrained and ostensibly obedient, lions would appear to lie down in humility in front of the emperor.

However, Khan was venerated for much more than these acts of mere wizardry. Polo's account tells us that the ruler presided over an extremely modern state. Paper currency, integrated with seals of authenticity to prevent counterfeiting, existed during Khan's rule. In addition, his establishment of a vast postal system meant that he would receive news in a fraction of the time that was normally required. Under the rule of Khan, the roads of the empire were also well-maintained, and travelers could reach their destinations relatively quickly and efficiently.

5.   Which of the following best describes the organization of the passage?
    A. It discusses a problem and then provides a solution.
    B. It recounts a story and then offers an explanation.
    C. It compares one version of a historical event to a differing account and interpretation of the event.
    D. It gives the historical background to a piece of writing and then provides further details about it.

Look, I am clean out of ideas. I want to get to the bottom of this as much as you do, but at the end of the day, it's your problem not mine. I mean, I have problems of my own and my own life to live. Besides, what will our friends think when they find all of this out? Your parents and relatives are really bound to be shocked and upset too when they know. I mean, honestly, who wouldn't be? This is no way to live. You have to fess up to what you've done so you can say your apologies and make a clean start.

6.   The imperative to "say your apologies and make a clean start" is intended mainly to reinforce the narrator's:

A. view of his friend's parents.

B. frustration about how other people view his friend.

C. sense of urgency in helping his friend.

D. sense of empathy for his friend's relatives.

Painted by the Norwegian artist Edvard Munch, *The Scream* depicts the skeletal face of a person in clear psychological distress. Contrasted against a serene background of asymmetrical red and yellow swirls that represent the sunset, the desperation in the facial characteristics of the subject is said to express humanity's reaction to the anxieties of modern life. Completing the work at the age of 29, Munch admitted that he felt as if a scream went through himself during that time since he was in a state of poor mental and physical health while painting the piece.

7.   According to the passage, which one of the following factors most influenced Munch's painting of *The Scream*?

A. his age at the time of working on the painting

B. his own lack of psychological and physiological well-being

C. humanity's experiences of the anxieties of modern life

D. the asymmetry of his artistic technique

Gibberellins are a complex group of plant hormones that are involved in many botanical processes. Commonly used in combination with similar botanical hormones called auxins, their primary function is to promote plant growth by controlling the elongation of cells. They also promote the formation of fruit and seed, as well as delay aging in leaves. Having become important for commercial reasons in recent years, the hormones are also used to help meet the ever-growing demand for new hybrids of plants and flowers.

8.   Which of the following best summarizes the botanical significance of gibberellins?

A. Without them, plant hormones would be involved in more processes.

B. Because of gibberellins, plant cells enlarge, thereby causing plants to grow.

C. Leaves age more quickly, owing to the function of gibberellins.

D. Gibberellins have nocuous consequences for fruits and seeds.

Reconstruction is the process whereby words are constructed in an undocumented language by comparing its sound system to that of known related languages. The practice, which is also called internal reconstruction, is based on the postulation that certain sounds have variants in various languages. For instance, the Latin word "pater" and the Gothic word "fadar" show a systematic correspondence between the "p" and "f" sounds in these languages. This leads to the hypothesis that "p" was the earlier variant of the "f" consonant in other related languages, as well as in antediluvian languages and Indo-European forms.

9. Which of the following, if true, would most strengthen the argument presented in the passage?

A. The "f" sound was an early variant of the "p" sound in antediluvian languages.

B. Several languages around the world today remain undocumented.

C. The "c" and "k" sounds are easily distinguished from each other in many languages.

D. A systematic correspondence exists between the "b" and "v" sounds in certain languages.

For every building that is successfully constructed, there are countless others that have never received the chance to leave the drawing board. Some of these unbuilt structures were practical and mundane, while others expressed the flights of fancy of the architect. Known to us today only through the plans left on paper, many unbuilt buildings were originally designed to commemorate particular people or events. Such was the case with the monument dubbed the Beacon of Progress, which was to be erected in Chicago to display exhibits dedicated to great Americans in history. However, scholar Samantha Mulholland points out that other proposed projects "were far more quixotic, like that of The Floating Spheres, described as modules held aloft by hot air to house cities of the future."

10.   Which of the following best explains why the writer includes a quotation by Samantha Mulholland?

   A. to imply that some projects were never undertaken due to the fact that they did not commemorate any significant event

   B. to suggest that the plans for some projects had serious design flaws

   C. to demonstrate that some projects were too extravagant and impractical ever to be built

   D. to criticize people who were not ready to face the future of housing at the time that the construction of The Floating Spheres was proposed

A complex series of interactive patterns govern nearly everything the human body does. We eat to a rhythm and drink, sleep, and even breathe to separate ones. Research shows that the human body clock is affected by three main rhythmic cycles: the rhythm at which the earth revolves on its axis, the monthly revolution of the moon around the earth, and the annual revolution of the earth around the sun. These rhythms create a sense of time that is both physiological as well as mental. Humans feel hungry about every four hours, sleep about eight hours in every 24-hour period, and dream in cycles of approximately 90 minutes each.

These natural rhythms, sometimes called circadian rhythms, are partially controlled by the hypothalamus in the brain. Circadian rhythms help to explain the "lark vs. owl" hypothesis. Larks are those who prefer to rise early in the morning and go to bed early, while owls are those who feel at their best at night. These cycles explain the phenomenon of jet lag, when the individual's body clock is out of step with the actual clock time in his or her new location in the world. In humans, births and deaths also follow predictable cycles, with most births and deaths occurring between midnight and 6:00 am.

11. The author would most likely recommend that sufferers of jet lag do which of the following?

    A. Better control their circadian rhythms.

    B. Take medicine to regulate the hypothalamus.

    C. Go to bed earlier than usual.

    D. Allow their body clocks to adjust to the time difference naturally.

The ancient legal code of Babylonia had severe sanctions for a wide range of crimes. Perhaps best viewed as a way to express personal vengeance, punishments included cutting off the fingers of boys who had hit their fathers or gouging out the eyes of those who had blinded another person. As with most ancient peoples, the Babylonians did not believe in humane treatments for offenders. Sumerian King Ur Nammu, who formulated a set of laws that were surprisingly modern in their approach, did not follow these draconian forms of retribution. Sumerian law stipulated that perpetrators of violent crimes pay monetary damages to their victims, and Ur Nammu's system is the first recorded example of financial awards being imposed in lieu of other forms of punishment.

12. The author mentions Sumerian King Ur Nammu primarily in order to:

A. provide a contrast with the forms of punishment meted out by the Babylonians.

B. criticize previous Babylonian rulers.

C. emphasize the severity of the Babylonian system of justice.

D. imply that Babylonian sanctions were just for their time.

Depicting the events of a single day, James Joyce's epic novel *Ulysses* took more than 20,000 hours, or a total of eight years, to write. Set in Dublin, the novel was initially published in installments as a series before the Parisian publishing house Shakespeare and Company issued a limited edition of 1,000 copies. The book was risqué for its time, and was classified as obscene material in the United Stated. After the work was cleared of obscenity charges, an unexpurgated version was accepted for publication by Random House in New York. Ironically, it was not available in Dublin until 40 years later.

13. It can reasonably be concluded from the passage that the writer of the article would argue that *Ulysses* was published in Dublin 40 years after it was released in New York because:

   A. Irish publishing companies often engage in dilatory practices when dealing with their authors.

   B. Irish publishers were dissuaded in publishing the novel since it depicted the events of only one day.

   C. Social mores in Dublin were much stricter than those of the United States at that time.

   D. Dublin had a more liberal society than that of Paris.

Questions 14 to 16 refer to the following pair of passages.

Passage 1:

Resulting from the amazing success of WAP (Wireless Application Protocol) in smart phones and hand-held devices, wireless technology can have an amazing impact on your day-to-day life. These technologies help to make the mobile information society happen by blurring the boundaries between home, the office, and the outside world.

The seamless integration and connectivity that wireless technology brings with it make it possible to work more efficiently. Business users can explore a wide range of interactive services which were difficult to envisage years ago because of the complexity involved in making such devices communicate with each other.

In addition, with wireless technologies, you can get on social media wherever you are, helping us stay connected with friends and family.

Passage 2:

Recent research shows that social media platforms may actually be making us antisocial. Survey results indicate that many people would prefer to interact on Facebook or Twitter, rather than see friends and family in person. The primary reason cited for this phenomenon was that one does not need to go to the effort to dress up and travel in order to use these social media platforms.

Another independent survey revealed that people often remain glued to their hand-held devices when they do go out with friends. It therefore seems that social media platforms may be having a detrimental effect on our social skills and interpersonal relationships.

14.   The writer of Passage 1 would most likely criticize the writer of Passage 2

   for:

   A. relying on research results rather than anecdotal information.

   B. placing too much emphasis on certain social media platforms.

   C. talking about hand-held devices in particular, rather than wireless

       technology in general.

   D. overlooking the positive effect that wireless technologies have had on

       work and office life.

15.   The writer of Passage 2 would probably respond to the last sentence in

   Passage 1 (In addition, . . . family.) by:

   A. asserting that one should try to balance time spent on social media

       platforms with time spent in person with loved ones.

   B. pointing out that social media platforms are very convenient.

   C. claiming that we are actually damaging relationships with our friends

       and family in many cases because of wireless technologies.

   D. arguing that people should leave their hand-held devices at home

       when going out with friends.

16.   The writers of both passages would agree that:

   A. wireless technologies have impacted upon society in positive ways.

   B. social media platforms need to be used with caution.

   C. social media platforms have brought about changes to interpersonal

   relationships.

   D. Facebook and Twitter are useful interactive tools for business users.

Educational psychology studies pupils in a classroom setting in order to help educators to understand the behaviors and attitudes that affect learning and teaching. This branch of psychology was a reaction against the psychometric movement, which tested students in order to place them into "streamed" classes of different ability levels. The popularity of IQ testing and streamed education declined in the second half of the twentieth century, and the education profession is now focused on developing programs that view students as individuals and advising schools how better to function as organizations.

17. According to the passage, the best way to distinguish between the education profession before the second half of the twentieth century and current educational practice would be by:

A. looking at the results of psychometric testing.

B. studying pupils in a classroom setting.

C. supporting the benefits of IQ testing.

D. determining whether students are grouped into categories based on test results.

For any state to make sex a qualification that must ever result in the disfranchisement of one entire half of the people is a violation of the supreme law of the land. By it, the blessings of liberty are forever withheld from women and their female posterity. To them, this government has no just powers derived from the consent of the governed. To them, this government is not a democracy. It is not a republic. It is an *odious* aristocracy; a hateful *oligarchy* of sex; the oligarchs over the mother and sisters, the wife and daughters, of every household – which ordains all men *sovereigns*, all women subjects, carries dissension, discord, and rebellion into every home of the nation (Excerpt from "On Women's Right to Vote" by Susan B. Anthony).

18.   The use of the words "odious," "oligarchy," and "sovereigns" serves to support the argument that:

A.   the entire populace is disenfranchised.

B.   the government is too powerful.

C.   the situation is unfair and change is necessary.

D.   dissension and rebellion are bound to increase.

19.   Working under great secrecy, the group had to limit access to the details

of their _____ plan.

    A. loquacious

    B. covert

    C. terse

    D. tantamount

20.   If only the snow would _____ for a few days, they could clear a pass

through the mountains.

    A. stop short

    B. tread lightly

    C. hold off

    D. hold back

Accuplacer Reading Practice Test 2 – Answers

1. B

2. A

3. C

4. A

5. D

6. C

7. B

8. B

9. D

10. C

11. D

12. A

13. C

14. D

15. C

16. C

17. D

18. C

19. B

20. C

Accuplacer Reading Practice Test 2 – Answers and Explanations

1. The correct answer is B. The passage explains how Mr. Morris conformed to social convention throughout his life. We can see this idea, for example, at the end of paragraph 1, which states: "Everything that it was right and proper for a man in his position to possess, he possessed." This idea is repeated at the beginning of paragraph 4, in the statement that: "He underwent various changes according to the accepted custom in these cases."

2. The correct answer is A. Paragraph 2 describes how Mr. Morris had "the right sort and number of children." So, the reader can assume that Mr. Morris's children, like Mr. Morris himself, conform to social convention by trying to be responsible and logical. In other words, they are not highty-flighty or empty-headed.

3. The correct answer is C. The narrator tells us that Mr. Morris's home was "a nice sensible house," and his tomb is described as "being the fashion of his time." The reader can therefore deduce that both the house and the tomb would have been considered right and proper for the society of their time.

4. The correct answer is A. The reader can conclude that the story is going to be about how life in the future is different than life in the past because it talks about both the past and the future in the last paragraph of the passage. In addition, the word "future" is capitalized in one instance to give emphasis to this concept.

5. The correct answer is D. The passage gives the historical background to a piece of writing and then provides further details about it. Paragraph 1 describes the book *Il Milione*, and paragraph 2 provides some additional information about Polo's written account of events.

6. The correct answer is C. We can understand the sense of urgency that the narrator feels when he says: "This is no way to live."

7. The correct answer is B. Munch's own lack of psychological and physiological well-being most influenced his painting of *The Scream*. The last sentence of the passage explains that "Munch admitted that he felt as if a scream went through himself during that time since he was in a state of poor mental and physical health while painting the piece." Note that "physiological" and "physical" are synonyms.

8. The correct answer is B. Gibberellins are of botanical significance because they cause plant cells to enlarge, thereby causing plants to grow. The passage states that the primary function of gibberellins "is to promote plant growth by controlling the elongation of cells."

9. The correct answer is D. The discovery that a systematic correspondence exists between the *b* and *v* sounds in certain languages would most strengthen the argument presented in the passage. This correspondence would be similar to the "systematic correspondence between the *p* and *f* sounds in these languages," which is mentioned in the passage.

10. The correct answer is C. Samantha Mulholland suggests some proposed projects were never constructed because they were too extravagant and impractical ever to be built. The passage states: "Scholar Samantha Mulholland points out other proposed projects were far more quixotic." The word "quixotic" means extravagant and impractical.

11. The correct answer is D. The author would most likely recommend that sufferers of jet lag allow their body clocks to adjust to the time difference naturally. The author begins the second paragraph by explaining that "these natural rhythms, sometimes called circadian rhythms, are partially controlled by the hypothalamus in the brain." Since the author refers to the rhythms as a natural phenomenon, he or she would most likely suggest that the time difference be overcome naturally

12. The correct answer is A. The author mentions Sumerian King Ur Nammu primarily in order to provide a contrast with the usual forms of punishment meted out by the Babylonians. The passage states that "the Babylonians did not believe in humane treatments for offenders." However, King Ur Nammu "did not follow these draconian forms of retribution."

13. The correct answer is C. The author suggests that social mores in Dublin were much stricter than those of the United States at the time that Ulysses was published in New York. The passage tells us that "the book was risqué for its time" and was originally classified as "obscene material." In this

context, the word "mores" means moral views, and the word "risqué" means indecent.

14. The correct answer is D. The writer of passage 1 talks about office life in paragraph 1 and about business users in paragraph 2. The writer of passage 2 does not mention these aspects of wireless technology.

15. The correct answer is C. The writer of passage 2 explains how people are more inclined to stay at home to chat on social media than to go out with friends and how people are glued to their hand-held devices even when they are out with friends. These are two detrimental impacts of social media on interpersonal relationships.

16. The correct answer is C. The writer of passage 1 describes the positive changes, while the writer of passage 2 describes the negative changes.

17. The correct answer is D. According to the passage, the best way to distinguish between the education profession before the second half of the twentieth century and current educational practice is by determining whether students are grouped into categories based on test results. The passage explains that students used to be placed "into 'streamed' classes of different ability levels." However, current educational practice is to "view students as individuals."

18. The correct answer is C. "Odious" means hated or detestable; "oligarchy" refers to a dominant group, and "sovereign" means powerful. In addition, "disenfranchise" in the first sentences means to deprive individuals of their

rights. So, the author is arguing that men have power over women and that this situation is unfair to women.

19. The correct answer is B. "Covert" refers to something that is done in secret.

20. The correct answer is C. With reference to the weather, "hold off" means fail to occur or stop.

Accuplacer Reading Practice Test 3

Questions 1 to 4 refer to the following passage.

It was the last day of July. The long hot summer was drawing to a close; and we, the weary pilgrims of the London pavement, were beginning to think of the cloud-shadows on the corn-fields, and the autumn breezes on the sea-shore.

For my own poor part, the fading summer left me out of health and out of spirits. During the past year I had not managed my professional resources as carefully as usual; and my extravagance now limited me to the prospect of spending the autumn economically between my mother's cottage at Hampstead and my own chambers in town.

The evening, I remember, was still and cloudy. It was one of the two evenings in every week which I was accustomed to spend with my mother and my sister. So I turned my steps northward in the direction of Hampstead.

The quiet twilight was still trembling on the topmost ridges of the heath; and the view of London below me had sunk into a black gulf in the shadow of the cloudy night, when I stood before the gate of my mother's cottage. I had hardly rung the bell before the house door was opened violently; my worthy Italian friend, Professor Pesca, appeared in the servant's place and darted out joyously to receive me, with a shrill foreign parody on an English cheer.

I had first become acquainted with my Italian friend by meeting him at certain great houses where he taught his own language and I taught drawing. All I then knew of the history of his life was that he had once held a situation in the

University of Padua, that he had left Italy for political reasons (the nature of which he uniformly declined to mention to any one), and that he had been for many years respectably established in London as a teacher of languages.

I had seen him risk his life in the sea at Brighton. We had met there accidentally, and were bathing together. It never occurred to me that the art which we were practicing might merely add one more to the list of manly exercises which the Professor believed that he could learn impromptu. (Excerpt from *The Woman in White* by Wilkie Collins)

1.   What does the narrator suggest in paragraph 2?

    A. that he has run out of money

    B. that he has lost all his clients

    C. that he is suffering from depression

    D. that he does not get along well with his mother

2.   Why does the narrator mention his mother and sister in paragraph 3?

    A. to imply that Hampstead is in a poorer part of the city

    B. to foreshadow the events that will take place in his mother's cottage

    C. to indicate a routine

    D. to create a contrast with Professor Pesca

3.   Based on the passage, which of the following most accurately summarizes the following phrase from paragraph 4?: "appeared in the servant's place"

    A. rang the bell for the doorman

    B. did the job of the doorman

C. stood where the servant normally stands

D. received the servant's guests

4. The narrator most strongly suggests which of the following in the last paragraph?

A. Professor Pesca saved someone who was drowning.

B. Professor Pesca was not prone to impulsive actions.

C. Professor Pesca did not know how to swim.

D. Professor Pesca had experience working with the Coast Guard.

We stand today at the threshold of a great event both in the life of the United Nations and in the life of mankind, that is the approval by the General Assembly of the Declaration of Human Rights. This declaration may well become the international Magna Carta of all people everywhere. We hope its proclamation by the General Assembly will be an event comparable to the proclamation of the Declaration of the Rights of Man by the French people in 1789, the adoption of the Bill of Rights by the people of the United States, and the adoption of comparable declarations at different times in other countries (Excerpt from "Adoption of the Declaration of Human Rights" by Eleanor Roosevelt).

5. The speaker most likely mentions the Magna Carta, the Declaration of the Rights of Man, and the Bill of Rights in order to:

   A. incite dissent among the audience members.

   B. emphasize the historical importance of this event.

   C. persuade her opponents to support this declaration.

   D. predict future proclamations by the General Assembly.

Questions 6 to 10 refer to the following pair of passages.

Passage 1:

Abraham Lincoln observed that happiness is a choice for most people. This echoes the claims of the Dalai Lama, who stated that people can decide whether they will be happy or not through self-discipline. So, isn't the choice simple really? Shouldn't we choose to be happy? Being happy occurs when we choose not to worry. This choice is based on a thankful attitude. We have so much to be thankful for. Thank the taxi driver for bringing you home safely, thank the cook for a wonderful dinner, and thank the person who cleans your windows. When we give thanks to others whenever possible, we choose the path of gratitude that leads to the road to happiness.

Passage 2:

Almost everyone has heard the hit single "Don't Worry, Be Happy" by Bobby McFerrin. But isn't McFerrin's refrain that everyone can choose to be happy by simply deciding not to worry overly simplistic in reality? Living a happy and worry-free life is a wonderful ideal, but it must be said that life is full of stresses and strains that are often not of our own choosing. One of the truest things ever said is that the only thing in life that will always remain the same is change. In addition to causing us to worry, stress is linked to the top causes of death, such as heart disease, cancer, and stroke. So, achieving happiness in today's society is often a complex, multi-dimensional process.

6.	Which of the following statements best describes the relationship between Passage 1 and Passage 2?

  A. Passage 1 introduces a theory that is supported by the examples in Passage 2.

  B. Passage 1 explains a philosophy that conflicts with the personal anecdote recounted in Passage 2.

  C. Passage 1 describes a problematic situation that is ameliorated by the remedy described in Passage 2.

  D. Passage 2 provides an argument that undermines the viewpoint expressed in Passage 1.

7.	With which of the following ideas do both authors agree?

  A. Happiness is the result of decisions we make.

  B. Most people are not thankful enough.

  C. Many people lack of self-discipline.

  D. Worry has a direct impact on happiness.

8.	The use of the phrase "choose to be happy" in both passages serves to:

  A. convey two differing opinions on whether a happy, worry-free life can really be achieved.

  B. emphasize the view that the decisions that people make have the greatest influence on their lives.

  C. demonstrate both authors' support for the idea that happiness is a choice.

D. illustrate the disagreement over how people should express their gratitude.

9. How would the writer of Passage 1 most likely respond to the following statement from Passage 2?: "It must be said that life is full of stresses and strains that are often not of our own choosing."

A. People who experience stress are ungrateful for the positive aspects of their lives.

B. Abraham Lincoln and the Dalai Lama also experienced stress.

C. It may be true that we cannot choose certain events in life, but we can still choose to be happy.

D. Stressed-out people lack self-discipline generally.

10. What can reasonably be concluded about the song "Don't Worry, Be Happy" by Bobby McFerrin?

A. It was an extremely popular song at that time.

B. Many people were opposed to the message that the song expressed.

C. The song elaborates on the changes and stresses in one's life.

D. The song addresses the fact that life is full of events that are not of our own choosing.

In December of 1880, a friend who was a veterinary surgeon gave Louis Pasteur two rabid dogs for research purposes. Victims of bites from rabid dogs normally showed no symptoms for three to twelve weeks. By then, however, the patient would be suffering from convulsions and delirium, and it would be too late to administer any remedy.

So-called treatments at that time consisted of burning the bitten area of skin with red-hot pokers or with carbolic acid. Pasteur devoted himself to discovering a more humane and effective method of treatment for the disease. His tests on the rabid dogs confirmed that rabies germs were isolated in the saliva and nervous systems of the animals. After many weeks of tests and experiments, Pasteur cultivated a vaccine. Derived from a weakened form of the rabies virus itself, the vaccine is administered before the microorganism is encountered and stimulates the immune system to recognize and fight off any future exposure to the organism.

11. Which of the following situations provides the closest example to the use of a vaccine, as it is described in the passage?

  A. a patient who is given an antibiotic to recover from an infection

  B. a person who gargles every day in the belief that it will help prevent catching a cold

  C. a person who takes medicine after having been told she has high cholesterol

  D. children who get injections to prevent catching mumps and measles

"Celebrity" is the term used to describe someone who is famous and attracts attention from the general public and the world's media. Traditionally, a celebrity would gain the title by his or her work or achievements in a particular field of expertise. Actors, musicians, politicians, and inventors have all become celebrities in the past. However, as the twenty-first century progresses, a new celebrity has arrived—the nobody. As one peruses glossy TV magazines, it is easy to notice the amount of reality shows that now dominate our screens—*Wife Swap*, *American Idol*, *America's Got Talent*, and the reality pioneer *Big Brother*. The concept itself of *Big Brother* is everything that George Orwell warned us about: "normal" people are thrust into the limelight to be mocked, glorified, vilified, and humiliated in equal measures. And we lap it up.

12.   The writer would most strongly agree with which one of the following claims?

A. Reality TV participants are so-called celebrities who have no real achievements or expertise.

B. Reality TV participants are foolish for wanting to appear on television.

C. The general public needs to stop watching reality TV shows in order to prevent the phenomenon of spurious celebrity.

D. Glossy TV magazines should stop promoting reality TV shows.

"All knowledge that is about human society, and not about the natural world, is historical knowledge, and therefore rests upon judgment and interpretation. This is not to say that facts or data are non-existent, but that facts get their importance from what is made of them in interpretation, for interpretations depend very much on who the interpreter is, who he or she is addressing, what his or her purpose is, and at what historical moment the interpretation takes place" (Excerpt from *Culture and Imperialism*, Edward Said).

13.   The primary purpose of the passage is to:

   A. assert that historical knowledge diverges from knowledge about nature.

   B. emphasize the historical significance of facts and data.

   C. argue that historical knowledge hinges on analyses and opinions.

   D. point out that historical knowledge is dubious from an academic perspective.

Michelangelo began work on the massive project of painting of the ceiling of the Sistine Chapel in Italy in the summer of 1508, assisted by six others who helped to mix his paint and plaster. However, as work proceeded, the artist dismissed each of his assistants one by one, claiming that they lacked the competence necessary to do the task at hand. Described as the lonely genius, the painter himself often felt incompetent to complete the project entrusted to him by Pope Julius II. Having trained as a sculptor, Michelangelo had an extremely low opinion of his own painting skills. Yet, he went on to paint one of the most beautiful works in art history. In spite of his frequent personal misgivings, he persevered to paint the ceiling with his vision of the creation of the universe. The nine series of scenes that he painted include the Separation of Light from Darkness, the Drunkenness of Noah, the Ancestors of Christ, and the Salvation of Mankind.

14. Which of the following statements best represents the organization of the passage?

    A. Michelangelo's artistic background and temperament are described before going on to describe the importance of his achievement.

    B. The customs and manners of the past are summed up before moving on to the present viewpoints on Michelangelo's art.

    C. An assertion about the historical importance of Michelangelo's work is provided before expounding on this claim.

    D. Michelangelo's character traits are explained before describing artistic trends in general.

(1) The Higgs mechanism is the process in quantum field theory whereby symmetry is broken down, leading to massive particles. **(2)** Quantum field theory alone tells us that all particles should be massless. **(3)** Yet, groundbreaking scientific research has found that particles can acquire mass when the symmetry of energy within a system is less than that of the interaction governing the system. **(4)** Theoretically, scientists now understand that the Higgs particle is a by-product of the acquisition of mass by other particles. **(5)** Discovering this elusive particle remains one of the greatest challenges of modern-day particle physicists.

15. The third sentence in the passage marks a shift from facts about quantum field theory to:

A. the subject of the relationship between mechanisms and particles.

B. the revelation that the Higgs mechanism inheres in a basic contradiction.

C. the illustration of how the symmetry of energy within a system can be lower than that of the governing system.

D. the refutation of the notion that particles can be by-products of mass.

The other children were shouting out at me, calling my name and begging me to stop. But I didn't. I ran all the way past them, down the street, past the garbage cans, and towards our house. I kept running and didn't even start to slow down until I saw my mom on the front porch. She was sitting there wearing that pretty flowered dress that I like and smiling at me, with her eyes full of love. We have had our ups and downs lately – I know it sounds odd me saying that in the circumstances – but she has always been my best ally and the one person that I can really count on when times get tough.

16. When the narrator says, "I know it sounds odd me saying that in the circumstances," she mostly likely means that:

   A. her mother can also be quite tough on her at times.

   B. she realizes that her mother should have been upset or angry at her.

   C. she understands that the reader may find it contradictory to her description of her mother's love.

   D. she knows that running down the street was the wrong thing to do.

According to Stephen Krashen's input hypothesis, a language learner improves his or her language skills when he or she is exposed to language input such as lectures or reading materials that are one level above the learner's current level of language ability. Language output such as verbal or written expressions are not seen to have any direct effect on the learner's ability.

17. According to the passage, which of the following is the best summary of the input hypothesis?

A. It is an assumption that all language learners begin at the same level of ability.

B. It is a theory which asserts that learners can best improve their language skills when their learning is appropriately challenging.

C. It is a school of thought that discounts the importance of traditional grammatical skills.

D. It is a system of language rules established by Stephen Krashen that learners of new languages try to follow.

Do mice really prefer cheese to all other foodstuffs? One well-known American exterminator has revealed his secret to catching these pesky rodents: lemon-flavored candy. It appears that the confection has a double advantage. Its sweet smells attracts the mouse much more strongly than does cheese, and its sticky consistency helps to hold the creature captive for the moment it takes for the trap to release. Through logical analogy, we can therefore conclude that it is fallacious to presume that other groups of animals have stereotypical preferences for certain food groups. For instance, we cannot readily conclude that all dogs would choose meat or that all cats would select milk as their favorite foodstuffs.

18.   Which of the following, if true, would most strongly suggest that the logical analogy mentioned in the passage is incorrect?

A. Mice are attracted more to the texture of the candy than to its smell.

B. Some animals have a very acute sense of smell.

C. Many scientific experiments demonstrate that dogs do not prefer the taste and texture of meat to the taste and texture of other food.

D. Independent observations reveal that mice eat cheese as often as they lemon-flavored candy when both foodstuffs are available to them at the same time.

19.	Emotions were running high, and the situation was _____ with

	stress and tension.

	A.	fraught

	B.	manifest

	C.	clandestine

	D.	impacted

20.	The professor's explanation was just too complicated. I couldn't

	_____ what she was trying to explain.

	A.	jettison

	B.	fathom

	C.	beckon

	D.	kindle

Accuplacer Reading Practice Test 3 – Answers

1. A

2. C

3. B

4. C

5. B

6. D

7. D

8. A

9. C

10. A

11. D

12. A

13. C

14. A

15. B

16. C

17. B

18. D

19. A

20. B

Accuplacer Reading Practice Test 3 – Answers and Explanations

1. The correct answer is A. The narrator states in paragraph 2 that he needs to spend the autumn "economically," so the reader can surmise that he is having financial problems. Note that the narrator mentions that he is "out of spirits," but this condition is not as serious as suffering from depression.

2. The correct answer is C. The narrator says: "It was one of the two evenings in every week which I was accustomed to spend with my mother and my sister." The word "accustomed" indicates that a routine is being described.

3. The correct answer is B. The doorman would have been the servant who welcomed visitors at the front door of the house.

4. The correct answer is C. The last paragraph tells us that swimming was one of the "manly exercises which the Professor believed that he could learn impromptu." The word "impromptu" means "on the spot" or "without previous practice or experience."

5. The correct answer is B. The speaker most likely mentions the Magna Carta, the Declaration of the Rights of Man, and the Bill of Rights in order to emphasize the historical importance of this event. We can understand this attitude because the speaker begins her address by stating that "we stand today at the threshold of a great event."

6. The correct answer is D. Passage 2 provides an argument that undermines the viewpoint expressed in Passage 1. The first passage argues that people

can simply choose to be happy, but the second passage claims that "life is full of stresses and strains that are often not of our own choosing."

7. The correct answer is D. Both authors agree that worry has a direct impact on happiness. The author of passage 1 states that "being happy occurs when we choose not to worry." The author of passage 2 points out that worrying can lead to certain diseases which cause death.

8. The correct answer is A. The use of the phrase "choose to be happy" in both passages serves to convey two differing opinions on whether a happy, worry-free life can really be achieved. Passage 1 promotes happiness as a choice through the rhetorical questions: "So, isn't the choice simple really? Shouldn't we choose to be happy?" Passage 2 refutes this idea by posing another rhetorical question: But isn't McFerrin's refrain that everyone can choose to be happy by simply deciding not to worry overly simplistic in reality?"

9. The correct answer is C. The writer of Passage 1 would most likely respond to this statement by saying: "It may be true that we cannot choose certain events in life, but we can still choose to be happy." We can understand that the writer of passage 1 agrees with Abraham Lincoln's statement that "happiness is a choice for most people."

10. The correct answer is A. The writer states that "almost everyone has heard the song," so we can assume that it was very popular when the passage was written.

11. The correct answer is D. The closest example to the use of a vaccine, as it is described in the passage, is children who get injections to prevent catching mumps and measles. It is the only example from the answer choices involving taking medicine beforehand in order to prevent catching a disease.

12. The correct answer is A. The passage tells us that "traditionally, a celebrity would gain the title by his or her work or achievements in a particular field of expertise. [. . .] However, as the twenty-first century progresses, a new celebrity has arrived—the nobody." From these statements we can conclude that the writer is lamenting the fact that celebrities nowadays have no real achievements or expertise.

13. The correct answer is C. The passage states that "historical knowledge [. . .] rests upon judgment and interpretation. [. . .] Facts get their importance from what is made of them in interpretation." Interpretation is based on how something is analyzed, as well as the viewpoint of the interpreter. So, historical knowledge hinges on analyses and opinions.

14. The correct answer is A. Michelangelo's artistic background and temperament are described before going on to describe the importance of his achievement. The first four sentence describe the artist's personal characteristics and training, while the last three sentences talk about the artwork he created in the Sistine Chapel.

15. The correct answer is B. The author most likely mentions quantum field theory in the second sentence in order to reveal in the next sentence that the

Higgs mechanism inheres in a basic contradiction. In other words, quantum field theory tells us that all particles should be massless, but the Higgs mechanism shows that particles can acquire mass.

16. The correct answer is C. The narrator realizes that the reader may find it contradictory to her description of her mother's love. She has just said that "her mother's eyes were full of love" in spite of them having "ups and downs."

17. The correct answer is B. According to the passage, the best definition of the input hypothesis is that it is a theory which asserts that learners can best improve their language skills when their learning is appropriately challenging. The passage tells us that the learner should be exposed to "lectures or reading materials that are one level above the learner's current level of language ability." If the materials are a level above the learner's current level, they will challenge the learner.

18. The correct answer is D. The passage states: "Through logical analogy, we can therefore conclude that it is fallacious to presume that other groups of animals have stereotypical preferences for certain food groups." The logical analogy mentioned in the passage would be incorrect if it were true that mice eat cheese as often as they lemon-flavored candy when both foodstuffs are available to them at the same time. If the mice eat both food groups equally, they would not refute the stereotypical preference for cheese, and the logical analogy relies upon the refutation of this stereotypical preference.

19. The correct answer is A. The phrase "fraught with" means full of. It is often used to describe stressful situations.

20. The correct answer is B. The word "fathom" in this context means to understand or comprehend something.

Accuplacer Reading Practice Test 4

Questions 1 to 4 refer to the following passage.

Clare, restless, went out into the dusk when evening drew on, she who had won him having retired to her chamber. The night was as sultry as the day. There was no coolness after dark unless on the grass. Roads, garden-paths, the house-fronts, the bartonwalls were warm as earths, and reflected the noontime temperature into the noctambulist's face.

He sat on the east gate of the yard, and knew not what to think of himself. Feeling had indeed smothered judgement that day. Since the sudden embrace, three hours before, the twain had kept apart. She seemed stilled, almost alarmed, at what had occurred, while the novelty, unpremeditation, mastery of circumstance disquieted him—palpitating, contemplative being that he was. He could hardly realize their true relations to each other as yet, and what their mutual bearing should be before third parties thenceforward.

The windows smiled, the door coaxed and beckoned, the creeper blushed confederacy. A personality within it was so far-reaching in her influence as to spread into and make the bricks, mortar, and whole overhanging sky throb with a burning sensibility. Whose was this mighty personality? A milkmaid's.

It was amazing, indeed, to find how great a matter the life of this place had become to him. And though new love was to be held partly responsible for this, it was not solely so. Many have learnt that the magnitude of lives is not as to their external displacements, but as to their subjective experiences. The impressionable peasant leads a larger, fuller, more dramatic life than the king.

Looking at it thus, he found that life was to be seen of the same magnitude here as elsewhere.

Despite his heterodoxy, faults, and weaknesses, Clare was a man with a conscience. Tess was no insignificant creature to toy with and dismiss; but a woman living her precious life—a life which, to herself who endured or enjoyed it, possessed as great a dimension as the life of the mightiest to himself. Upon her sensations the whole world depended to Tess; through her existence all her fellow-creatures existed, to her. The universe itself only came into being for Tess on the particular day in the particular year in which she was born. (Excerpt from *Tess of the D'Ubervilles* by Thomas Hardy)

1.   The bartonwalls mentioned in paragraph 1 are most likely:

    A. an area in the garden.

    B. a feature of the natural landscape.

    C. a part of the house.

    D. a path leading to one of the roads.

2.   What is the meaning of the word "noctambulist" as it is used in the passage?

    A. a person who suddenly falls in love

    B. a person who responds impulsively to subjective experiences

    C. a person who experiences an external displacement

    D. a person who goes for a walk after dark

3. What is the best paraphrase of the following statement from paragraph 2: "what their mutual bearing should be before third parties thenceforward"?

    A. how they should behave to each other around other people

    B. whether or not they should support each other as a couple from this moment onwards

    C. whether or not they should kiss each other in public

    D. how they should decide whom to tell that they are now a couple

4. What does the narrator imply when he states that "Clare was a man with a conscience"?

    A. Clare has behaved poorly towards women in the past, but he repents of this behavior.

    B. Clare knows that Tess is hypersensitive, but she has to be aware of his needs.

    C. Clare understands that his life in his current environment may not be of the same magnitude that he has experienced in the past.

    D. Clare realizes that he needs to treat Tess well because she has had her own life experiences, both positive and negative.

Convection, which occurs because of changes in the density of a substance, is the process by which a liquid or gas rises and falls. For instance, when a liquid is heated, it will first rise in temperature and expand near the heat source. The warm fluid becomes less dense and rises as cold fluid falls to take its place. The rise of the warm liquid and the fall of the cool liquid in this way serve to transport or convect heat within the vessel. A similar convection process occurs in the heating and insulation of homes and other structures. Heating systems work by circulating warm air, which essentially serves to produce convection currents within a room.

5.   Based on the passage, which of the following most accurately characterizes the statement: "A similar convection process occurs in the heating and insulation of homes and other structures"?

A. a fact that can be substantiated by observation

B. a hypothesis that the speaker would like to prove

C. a doubt that has been dispelled in the speaker's mind

D. a claim that the speaker is trying to argue to the reader

Created by Ludwig Zamenhof to help overcome problems in international communication, Esperanto is perhaps the best known of the world's artificial languages. The Esperanto alphabet has 5 vowels and 23 consonants, which are derived mainly from the western European lexicon. The language also demonstrates the influence of Slavonic syntax and spelling.

It is extremely difficult to ascertain exactly how many people around the world use Esperanto, although estimates range from 1 million to 15 million users worldwide. Newspapers and magazines are published in Esperanto, and it is taught as a subject in academic institutions in several countries.

6. The second paragraph marks a shift in the passage from:

   A. describing facts about Esperanto's founder to explaining statistics about the users of the language.

   B. providing facts on the language itself to lamenting that it has so few users.

   C. giving a brief introduction on the creation and content of the language to talking about its uses worldwide.

   D. analyzing the language at a syntactical level to linking these factors to difficulties with learning the language.

The Atacama Desert in Chile is the driest place in the world. The average annual rainfall there is so low that it can't even be measured. But perhaps once every five or so years, it does rain there, and something truly miraculous takes place. "It was like stepping into paradise," remarked one visitor, who saw first-hand what the rains brought to the Atacama. She went on to describe in vivid detail "the beautiful, delicate flowers growing in gigantic swathes of color, as if the universe had cast millions of seeds into the wind." In fact, the flowers grow from the seeds left lying in the sand since the time of the desert's last blooming. Having a life cycle of only two weeks, these desert ephemerals germinate only when completely saturated with water, before flowering, withering, and dropping more seed.

7. In the passage, the use of the words "paradise," "beautiful," "delicate," and "swathes of color" serve mainly to emphasize:

    A. the visitor's sense of dramatic effect in describing the flowers that she saw.

    B. the visitor's claim that "It was like stepping into paradise."

    C. the writer's statement that "the rainfall is so low that it can't even be measured."

    D. the writer's intention to contrast the starkness of the desert to the beauty of the flowers.

It is ironic that the man who made such a great deal of money by bringing so much destruction to the world should dedicate the fortune he made to the promotion of peace. This man was Alfred Nobel, the inventor of dynamite and the founder of the Nobel Prize. Nobel later discovered that nitroglycerin could safely be absorbed into a form of silica and molded into sticks. This invention, which he named dynamite, was an enormous commercial success, and Nobel built ninety-three factories in several countries throughout the world.

During his lifetime, Nobel was concerned about how peace could be established among nations, and his will stipulated that the bulk of his fortune should be distributed annually in the form of prizes to those who had conferred the greatest benefit on humankind. Despite its aim to promote peace, however, the prize has sometimes produced competition that has brought out the worst in people. Scientists have been known to speed up or delay the publication of their research in order to be eligible for the prize in a particular year, and secrecy and unhealthy competition have also sprung up in the literary community. It seems that some of the worst aspects of human nature continue to exist, in spite of Nobel's intention to bring out the very best in humanity.

8. Which choice best describes the overall structure of the passage?

    A. Events are recounted in reserve chronological order

    B. The background to and intention of a philanthropist's bequest are compared to the occasional unfortunate outcomes of the bequest.

    C. Two achievements of a notable individual are compared and contrasted.

    D. Historical background to a subject is followed by a list of disadvantages.

A huge success worldwide in fast food restaurants such as McDonalds, Burger King, Pizza Hut, and Subway, franchising is the process whereby a license is granted to carry out a business activity, giving permission to use the name, trademark, products, commercial recognition, and know-how of the franchisor. The franchise holder has to agree to conform to the franchisor's standards and pay a franchise fee, which consists of an up-front payment plus a percentage of annual sales revenue. Franchise holders are usually only too happy pay this fee to get immediate name recognition, building design and decoration, and tried and tested techniques in running and promoting the business.

9.   Which of the following does the author provide as evidence for his assertion that franchise holders are "only too happy" to pay their franchise fees?

A. The description of the things that the franchise holder receives in exchange for his or her payment.

B. A list of well-known restaurants that operate on the franchise system.

C. The emphasis on the fact that a license must be granted in order to carry out business.

D. The basis of the agreement to operate and conform to the franchisor's standards.

Cars built today have one major advantage over those of the past: the use of plastic body panels. Plastic is resilient and can sometimes even bounce back after the car has experienced a minor collision. In contrast to steel and other metal amalgams, plastic is resistant to rust and corrosion. Plastic also makes the vehicle lightweight, meaning that it is more aerodynamic and fuel efficient. Further, plastic panels can be made in a wide variety of colors.

10. The passage most strongly emphasizes which advantage of the use of plastic car body panels?

   A. Plastic car body panels come in a variety of colors.

   B. Plastic car panels are more durable than those made from steel and metal amalgams.

   C. The use of plastic for car panels can result in less running costs to the car owner.

   D. Plastic car panels seldom get damaged in collisions.

Questions 11 to 14 refer to the following pair of passages.

Passage 1:

Diners in restaurants sometimes ask why their servers aren't able to cope with some of their requests. Is it fair to suggest that members of the service industry typically deliver below-par service to customers? Consider a simple example of a fast food restaurant. Chances are that you've been at the receiving end of some bad service at some point in time. Is it then fair to assume that work performance can be predicted by the clothes that workers wear or that staff who wear work uniforms are simply to be tagged with a warning sign that they will not deliver to their clientele?

To understand the reasons for occasional bad service, the factors influencing the situation need to be considered. Perhaps the person providing the service was new to his or her job. Maybe he or she was a trainee and was not able to perform without the assistance of a supervisor. In addition, service people can experience a great deal of stress when trying to do several things at once for different patrons.

Passage 2:

Whether in the fast food service or in a legal firm, there are countless factors that can influence the outcome of the service provided. However, a person who wears a suit to work is less likely to make a mistake than someone in the service industry. The hurried pace and pressure to perform in the service industry cause mistakes to occur. Those who do office work have the luxury of working in less stressful environments. They have more time to check their work for mistakes before delivering it to their clients.

11. Which choice best describes the relationship between the two passages?

    A. Passage 1 incites the reader to evaluate the reasons for the poor service they have received, while passage 2 compares the factors that can affect employee performance in two different environments.

    B. Passage 1 focuses on asking thought-provoking questions to the reader about bad service, while passage 2 criticizes those who provide poor service.

    C. Passage 1 mainly discusses bad service in the fast food industry, while passage 2 analyzes other service firms.

    D. Passage 1 evaluates below-par service from the point of view of the customer, while passage 2 emphasizes the viewpoints of employees.

12. The writer of passage 1 would probably take the most offense with which one of the following claims from passage 2?

    A. Whether in the fast food service or in a legal firm, there are countless factors that can influence the outcome of the service provided.

    B. A person who wears a suit to work is less likely to make a mistake than someone in the service industry.

    C. The hurried pace and pressure to perform in the service industry cause mistakes to occur.

    D. Those who do office work have the luxury of working in less stressful environments.

13. How would the writer of passage 2 most likely respond to the following rhetorical question from passage 1: "Is it then fair to assume that work performance can be predicted by the clothes that workers wear or that staff who wear work uniforms are simply to be tagged with a warning sign that they will not deliver to their clientele?"

   A. This question is based on a fair assumption because service people generally make a great deal of mistakes in their work.

   B. This question is not based on a fair assumption because service people can't help making mistakes due to the fact that they are usually untrained.

   C. The assumption is not entirely unfounded because service people sometimes make mistakes owing to the fact that they don't have sufficient time to check their work.

   D. This question is based on an unfair assumption since work uniforms have no relationship to job performance.

14. The writers of both passages would agree that:

   A. office workers are less likely to make mistakes than service people.

   B. lawyers work more conscientiously than wait staff.

   C. the clothes a person wears can affect work performance.

   D. the service industry can be extremely stressful at times.

The experience of music today is diverging from that of the past. The use of streaming and downloading platforms has made it easy for music lovers to build digital music libraries to suit their own tastes. Gone are the days of waiting for a vinyl album to be manufactured since a video or sound file can now be uploaded by a singer and downloaded by the user in seconds. Music users can access million of new songs instantly and even experiment with different musical genres.

15. Which of the following would be the most similar to the examples provided in the passage?

A. Patients can get consultations with doctors online in order to diagnose their illnesses.

B. Students can download books and videos for free for particular topics and specific academic subjects.

C. A person can keep a private blog as a record of his or her daily thoughts.

D. Personal videos can be uploaded to various online platforms.

One simple microorganism is responsible for combating both world hunger and air pollution, is an ingredient in food coloring, and one day may even help to produce oxygen in space. The organism is safe and effective as a foodstuff and is very high in protein. This miracle organism is called Spirulina, a blue-green algae that is naturally found in certain lakes in America and Africa. Spirulina can also be manufactured in salt water, if it is feed the by-products from biogas generators. Biogas generators are a significant source of energy in parts of the world, but they normally have a serious environmental drawback: they produce large quantities of carbon dioxide. However, Spirulina consumes large quantities of the gas, making it the ideal crop to grow alongside biogas generators. Unfortunately, Spirulina has not been used as widely or researched as thoroughly as other nutritive organisms.

16.   It can reasonably be concluded from the passage that, in the author's opinion, Spirulina:

A. production should be made mandatory wherever biogas generators are in use.

B. should be exploited more widely in space exploration programs.

C. production should be limited in some cases because of the carbon dioxide it gives off.

D. should be grown and consumed when feasible as the foodstuff has beneficial outcomes for human health and quality of life.

I love Jonah, my best friend, but he is an absolute gossip. He always wants to know everything that is going on around town and can sometimes be a busybody. My mother says that he is a better source of information than the local radio station. I suppose he knows so much about everyone because he will just keep at you until you tell him everything, even if you didn't really want to or mean to. He is likable, even lovable when you get to know him, because he is so generous and has a big heart. Anyway, as the saying goes, "Nobody's perfect."

17.   The contrast that the narrator draws between his friend's shortcoming as "an absolute gossip" and the statement that his friend is "so generous and has a big heart" is most likely meant to emphasize that:

A. people would like Jonah even more than they do now if he gossiped a bit less.

B. the narrator's mother likes Jonah, in spite of having doubts about his character.

C. the narrator views his friend Jonah as lovable but imperfect.

D. people like Jonah because he pushes them to reveal their private information.

In her prolific writings as a novelist and philosopher, Iris Murdoch often describes the "just and loving gaze" that human beings should afford one another. In her philosophical tome entitled *Metaphysics as a Guide to Morals*, the writer explains that it is better to attempt the small act of kindness that is within one's capability and that one can therefore realistically achieve, rather than attempting a more grandiose moral act and failing at the gesture altogether. In other words, Murdoch warns against stretching out of reach in terms of one's own inner moral level. The characters of her novels, intelligent but hapless individuals who try (but fail) when "punching above their weight" when it comes to matters of ethics and morals, represent this phenomenon perfectly.

18.   Why does the writer use quotation marks around the phrase "punching above their weight"?

    A. to show that the phrase is not being used literally

    B. to express irony in her writing

    C. to cite the words attributed to another writer

    D. to indicate that the words were part of a dialogue

19.   The accident victim was lying _____ by the side of the road.

      A. prostrate

      B. abstemiously

      C. slovenly

      D. astray

20.   The sectarian group _____ the government currently in power

      and attempted to overthrow it.

      A. exalted

      B. assuaged

      C. repented

      D. renounced

Accuplacer Reading Practice Test 4 – Answers

1. C

2. D

3. A

4. D

5. A

6. C

7. D

8. B

9. A

10. C

11. A

12. B

13. C

14. D

15. B

16. D

17. C

18. A

19. A

20. D

Accuplacer Reading Practice Test 4 – Answers and Explanations

1.   The correct answer is C. The description moves from the roads, to the garden, and then to the house. In other words, the description moves from the outdoors to the house itself, so the bartonwalls are probably a part of the house.

2. The correct answer is D. Paragraph 1 mentions that it is after dusk and that it was nighttime. We also know from paragraph 1 that Clare was restless and that he had gone out.

3.   The correct answer is A. "Mutual bearing" means how they interact with each other. "Third parties" is a formal way of saying "other people."

4.   The correct answer is D. In the next sentence of the paragraph, the narrator tells us that "Tess was no insignificant creature to toy with and dismiss; but a woman living her precious life—a life which, to herself who endured or enjoyed it, possessed as great a dimension as the life of the mightiest to himself." This sentence describes both the positive and negative experiences in Tess's life. It implies that Clare needs to respect Tess when it states that she "was no insignificant creature to toy with and dismiss."

5.   The correct answer is A. The statement: "A similar convection process occurs in the heating and insulation of homes and other structures" is a fact that can be substantiated by observation. Anyone who has been in a heated room will notice how the air and heat circulate when the heating system is turned on.

6. The correct answer is C. The second paragraph marks a shift in the passage from giving a brief introduction on the creation and content of the language to talking about its uses worldwide. Paragraph 1 describes the contents of the alphabet, syntax, and spelling of the language, while Passage 2 states that the language is used in newspapers, magazines, and academic institutions.

7. The correct answer is D. The use of these words mainly emphasizes the writer's intention to contrast the starkness of the desert to the beauty of the flowers. The writer begins by describing how dry and inhospitable the desert is, before providing the visitor's description of the beautiful flowers.

8. The correct answer is B. The shift in the structure is indicated by the following sentence: "Despite its aim to promote peace, however, the prize has sometimes produced competition that has brought out the worst in people."

9. The correct answer is A. The writer mentions the things that the franchise holder receives in exchange for his or her payment, namely: "immediate name recognition, building design and decoration, and tried and tested techniques in running and promoting the business."

10. The correct answer is C. The writer mentions the resilience of plastic in minor accidents and its resistance to rust, as well as the fact that it makes the car more fuel efficient.

11. The correct answer is A. Passage 1 incites the reader to evaluate the reasons for the poor service they have received, especially in the examples

of lack of experience and training in paragraph 2. Passage 2 talks about the factors such as "the hurried pace" and the "stressful environments" that can affect service industry employee performance and compares this to that of office employees.

12. The correct answer is B. The writer of passage 1 poses the following rhetorical question: "Is it then fair to assume that work performance can be predicted by the clothes that workers wear or that staff who wear work uniforms are simply to be tagged with a warning sign that they will not deliver to their clientele?" She then goes on to refute this idea in the remainder of passage 1. Accordingly, the writer of passage 1 would disagree with the assertion from passage 2 that "a person who wears a suit to work is less likely to make a mistake than someone in the service industry."

13. The correct answer is C. The writer of passage 2 claims that "the hurried pace and pressure to perform in the service industry cause mistakes to occur." So, she would agree with the claim that those in the service industry sometimes do "not deliver to their clientele."

14. The correct answer is D. The writer of passage 1 mentions that "service people can experience a great deal of stress when trying to do several things at once for different patrons." The writer of passage 2 talks about "the hurried pace and pressure to perform in the service industry."

15. The correct answer is B. While all of the answer choices address activities that can be done online, answer B is the one that is most similar because it talks about downloading.

16. The correct answer is D. We know that the author holds the opinion that Spirulina is beneficial for human health and quality of life because the first sentence states that it "is responsible for combating both world hunger and air pollution." The writer goes on to emphasize: "The organism is safe and effective as a foodstuff and is very high in protein."

17. The correct answer is C. We know that the narrator views his friend Jonah as lovable but imperfect because he begins the passage by saying, "I love Jonah." We can also discern that he realizes that Jonah, like everyone, is imperfect because he ends the passage with the statement "Nobody's perfect."

18. The correct answer is A. The phrase "punching above their weight" is usually used in the sport of boxing. It is used in a nonliteral sense to describe someone who attempts something that he or she is not really capable of doing.

19. The correct answer is A. "Prostrate" means lying on the ground or lacking the will to rise up.

20. The correct answer is D. "Renounce" means to refuse to follow, obey, or recognize.

Accuplacer Reading Practice Test 5

Questions 1 to 4 refer to the following pair of passages.

Passage 1:

Good nutrition is essential for good health. A healthy diet can help a person to maintain a good body weight, promote mental wellbeing, and reduce the risk of disease. So, you might ask, what does good nutrition consist of? In my opinion, a healthy diet should include food from all of the major food groups. These food groups are carbohydrates, fruit, vegetables, dairy products, meat and other proteins, and fats and oils.

Passage 2:

For me, it is important to try to avoid processed or convenience food. Packaged food often contains chemicals, such as additives to enhance the color of the food or preservatives that give the food a longer life. Food additives are deleterious to health for a number of reasons. First of all, they may be linked to disease in the long term. In addition, they may block the body's ability to absorb the essential vitamins and minerals from food that are required for healthy bodily function.

1.   The passages most strongly emphasize which aspect of nutrition?

     A. Good health and wellbeing

     B. How to eat a balanced diet

     C. The basics of healthy eating

     D. The risks of food preservatives

2.   The tone and style of these passages most probably indicate that they

     both would be suitable for which of the following audiences?

     A. Adults listening to a radio program on nutrition

     B. Medical doctors attending a seminar

     C. Participants in a weight-loss support group

     D. College students in a biology lecture

3.   Which of the following words is closest in meaning to the word

     "deleterious" as it is used in passage 2?

     A. insipid

     B. harmful

     C. impeding

     D. provoking

4.   According to passage 2, what is the primary reason why manufacturers of

     processed food use additives?

     A. to make food more convenient

     B. to improve the appearance of the food

     C. to prevent the food from spoiling quickly

     D. to add nutrients to the food

She sighed in despair as he again showed no capacity to change his ways. "Why can't he see reason?" she wondered silently to herself for the umpteenth time that day.

The baby whimpered futilely in the next room, amid piles of unworn and unloved clothing. He too had learned that no matter how fiercely he cried, no one would come to his aid.

At times she felt like challenging her husband more strongly, or at least asking for an explanation of his behavior. Sadly, she too had been conditioned to learn that such actions were inutile. So, mute and hopeless, she stoically faced another day of domestic misery.

5. Which of the following most accurately characterizes the question "Why can't he see reason?" in the first paragraph of the passage?

   A. A lie that the narrator tells herself in order to keep calm

   B. A pessimistic outlook on a banal situation

   C. A question that the narrator feels she dare not ask her husband

   D. A necessary inquiry relevant to the daily lives of many people

6.   Which sentence from the passage best expresses its central idea?

   A. She sighed in despair as he again showed no capacity to change his ways.

   B. The baby whimpered futilely in the next room, amid piles of unworn and unloved clothing.

   C. He too had learned that no matter how fiercely he cried, no one would come to his aid.

   D. Sadly, she too had been conditioned to learn that such actions were useless.

7.   The words "inutile," "mute," and "hopeless" are mainly used to illustrate that the narrator feels:

   A. helpless

   B. useless

   C. impertinent

   D. pessimistic

8.   Which word below best describes the woman's behavior to her spouse?

   A. amiable

   B. volatile

   C. resigned

   D. futile

(1) Acid has been present in rain for millennia, naturally occurring from volcanoes and plankton. (2) However, scientific research shows that the acid content of rain has increased dramatically over the past two hundred years, in spite of humanity's recent attempts to control the problem.

(3) Rain consists of two elements, nitrogen and sulfur. (4) When sulfur is burned, it transforms into sulfur dioxide. (5) Nitrogen also oxides when burned. (6) When released from factories into the atmosphere, both sulfur dioxide and nitrogen oxide react with the water molecules in rain to form sulfuric acid and nitric acid, respectively.

(7) The acid in rain primarily emanates from automobile exhaust, domestic residences, and power stations. (8) The latter have been the culprit of the bulk of the acid in rainwater in recent years. (9) Since the pollutants are carried by the wind, countries can experience acid rain from pollution that was generated in countries thousands of miles away.

9. Which one of the following phrases provides the best summary of the phrase "the latter have been the culprit of the bulk" as it is used in sentence 8?

    A. Power stations have been the largest contributor to the problem.

    B. Automobile exhaust, domestic residences, and power stations have equally contributed to the creation of acid rain.

    C. Power stations are more widespread geographically than other causes of acid rain.

    D. Power stations generate a great deal of pollution that is carried by the wind.

The ancient Egyptians used eye shadow over 5,000 years ago. The cosmetic was used for personal beautification, as well as for practical reasons. Consisting of a paste made from malachite, a copper salt that was bright green, the eye paint protected against glare from the sun, in addition to being an attractive color. On her upper eye lids, Cleopatra wore blue eye shadow made of ground lapis lazuli stone, much like other women of her day.

The queen used green malachite as an accent below her eyes, and kohl, which consisted of lead sulfide, to provide color to her eyelashes and eyebrows. Red ochre, iron-based clay, provided her with lip and cheek color. Henna, a reddish-brown dye that was derived from a bush, was also commonly used by women in those days as a nail polish. The use of this particular cosmetic was not limited to women. Men also used the substance to darken their hair and beards.

10. Which of the following outlines best describes the overall structure of the topics addressed in paragraphs (1) and (2)?

A. **1.** Cosmetic uses of malachite; **2.** The beautification of Cleopatra

B. **1.** Cosmetics in ancient Egypt; **2.** Cosmetic uses of henna

C. **1.** The ancient Egyptians; **2.** The use of minerals in cosmetics

D. **1.** Ancient Egyptian eye shadow; **2.** Other ancient cosmetics

The notion of liberal arts education is believed to have been established in ancient Greece. Including the disciplines of logic, rhetoric, and grammar, a liberal arts education in those days was designed to train members of society to undertake important civic duties, such as jury service and public debate. In modern parlance, the term "liberal arts education" can be interpreted in a variety of ways, although it is generally taken to mean that the studies will include courses in one or more of the subject areas of the humanities, such as languages, literature, or philosophy.

11.   The passage provides information for most fully answering which of the following questions?

A. Why was liberal arts education originally established in Greece?

B. How did students study logic, rhetoric, and grammar in ancient times?

C. Why were jury service and public debate considered to be important civic duties?

D. What is the background to and definition of the term "liberal arts education"?

Ludwig von Beethoven was one of the most influential figures in the development of musical forms during the Classical period. Born in Bonn, Germany, the composer became a professional musician before the age of twelve. After studying under both Mozart and Haydn, Beethoven became a virtuoso pianist and had many wealthy patrons, who supported him financially. His most popular works are considered to be his fifth and sixth symphonies, and his only opera is entitled *Fidelio*. It is generally agreed that his compositions express the creative energy of the artist himself, rather than being written to suit the demands of his patrons.

12. The primary purpose of the passage is to:

    A. suggest that the works of Beethoven, Mozart, and Haydn are very similar.

    B. explore the development of musical composition during the Classical period.

    C. provide background information about Beethoven's life and work.

    D. explain how Beethoven acquired many wealthy patrons.

Around the world today, more than a billion people still do not have fresh, clean drinking water available on a daily basis. Hundreds of thousands of people in developing countries die needlessly every year because of the consumption of unclean, disease-ridden water. Simply stated, fresh water saves lives. However, what has been understood only recently is that the provision for fresh water around the globe also protects the environment because it means that those who manage water supplies must evaluate in more detail why and how developed countries consume and pollute their available water. Without this evaluation, an ever-increasing number of individuals will continue to die from water-related diseases.

13.   We can conclude from the information in this passage that:

A. water-related disease will decline in the future.

B. water-related deaths could be avoided.

C. children are the most vulnerable to water-related disease and death.

D. developed countries manage their water supplies better than developing countries.

Sir Isaac Newton had the prescience to appreciate that his study of natural phenomena was of great import for the scientific community and for society as a whole. It is because of Newton's work that we currently understand the effect of gravity on the earth as a global system. As a result of Newton's investigation into the subject of gravity, we know today that geological features such as mountains and canyons can cause variances in the Earth's gravitational force. Newton must also be acknowledged for the realization that the force of gravity becomes less robust as the distance from the equator diminishes, due to the rotation of the earth, as well as the declining mass and density of the planet from the equator to the poles.

14. What is the author's main purpose?

   A. to analyze natural phenomena

   B. to reconcile various gravitational theories

   C. to identify a reservation which Newton experienced

   D. to emphasize the significance of Newton's achievement

The use of computers in the stock market helps to control national and international finance. These controls were originally designed in order to create long-term monetary stability and protect shareholders from catastrophic losses. Yet, the high level of automation now involved in buying and selling shares means that computer-to-computer trading could result in a downturn in the stock market. Such a slump in the market, if not properly regulated, could bring about a computer-led stock market crash. For this reason, regulations have been put in place by NASDAQ, AMEX, and FTSE.

15. From this passage, one could infer that:

   A. regulations on computer-to-computer trading are considered to be a financial necessity.

   B. there are negative public views about regulations on computer-to-computer trading.

   C. NASDAQ, AMEX, and FTSE were initially opposed to establishing regulations on computer-to-computer trading.

   D. the role of computers in international markets has not been modified over time.

Born in France in 1896, Jean Piaget was one of the most influential thinkers in the area of child development in the twentieth century. Piaget posited that children go through a stage of assimilation as they grow to maturity. Assimilation refers to the process of transforming one's environment in order to bring about its conformance to innate cognitive schemes and structures. Schemes used in infant breast feeding and bottle feeding are examples of assimilation because the child utilizes his or her innate capacity for sucking to complete both tasks.

16.   Why does the writer mention bottle feeding in the above paragraph?

A. to identify one of the important features of assimilation

B. to exemplify the assimilation process

C. to describe the importance of assimilation

D. to explain difficulties children face during assimilation

Highly concentrated radioactive waste is lethal and can remain so for thousands of years. Accordingly, the disposal of this material remains an issue in most energy-producing countries around the world. In the United States, for example, liquid forms of radioactive waste are usually stored in stainless steel tanks. For extra protection, the tanks are double-walled and surrounded by a concrete covering that is one meter thick. This storage solution is also utilized the United Kingdom, in most cases.

The long-term problem lies in the fact that nuclear waste generates heat as radioactive atoms decay. This excess heat could ultimately result in a radioactive leak. Therefore, the liquid needs to be cooled by pumping cold water into coils inside the tanks. However, the tanks are only a temporary storage solution. The answer to the long-term storage of nuclear waste may be fusing the waste into glass cylinders that are stored deep underground.

17. Which of the following assumptions has most influenced the writer?

    A. The threat of a radioactive leak is exaggerated by the public.

    B. The storage of radioactive waste in stainless steel tanks is extremely dangerous.

    C. The United Kingdom normally follows practices that the United States has adopted.

    D. A radioactive leak would have disastrous consequences around the globe.

Born Marguerite Johnson, Maya Angelou was an American writer, poet, educator, and actor. Her seven autobiographies, based on her experiences of childhood and as a young adult, have been published around the world and have received international acclaim. From her writings, we know that Angelou was abused as a child and had a baby at sixteen, before going on to work as an actress and school administrator. Her writings are widely regarded as celebrating the African-American experience, as well as the capacity not only to survive hardship, but also to thrive and flourish in the face of adversity.

18.   The author mentions Angelou's childhood abuse most likely in order to:

    A. give an example of the hardship that she faced.

    B. provide a contrast to her work as a school administrator.

    C. reveal the main basis of her autobiographical writing.

    D. suggest the reason why she did not write under her real name.

19.   The judge lessened the sentence for the crime due to _____

      circumstances.

      A. mitigating

      B. implicating

      C. incriminating

      D. swindling

20.   No one could understand the _____ instructions.

      A. mawkish

      B. stalwart

      C. nebulous

      D. obsolete

Accuplacer Reading Practice Test 5 – Answers

1. C

2. A

3. B

4. B

5. C

6. D

7. A

8. C

9. A

10. D

11. D

12. C

13. B

14. D

15. A

16. B

17. D

18. A

19. A

20. C

Accuplacer Reading Practice Test 5 – Answers and Explanations

1. The correct answer is C. The passages most strongly emphasize the basics of healthy eating. This relates back to the rhetorical question in passage 1: "What does good nutrition consist of?"

2. The correct answer is A. The audience is most likely to be adults listening to a radio program on nutrition. The passages have conversational tones, beginning sentences with words like "so" and "well."

3. The correct answer is B. We know that the word "deleterious" has a negative connotation because the passage is talking about disease at this point, so "harmful" is the best synonym.

4. The correct answer is B. According to the passage, the primary reason why manufacturers of processed food use additives is to improve the appearance of the food. In the second sentence of Passage 2, we see that additives "enhance the color of food."

5.   The correct answer is C. The question is one that the narrator feels she dare not ask her husband directly. We know this because the narrator is described as "mute and hopeless" in the last sentence of the passage.

6. The correct answer is D. The following sentence from the passage best expresses its central idea: "Sadly, she too had been conditioned to learn that such actions were useless." The idea of conditioning is also mentioned in paragraph 2, with respect to the baby learning that crying would not change anything.

7. The correct answer is A. The woman sees that there is no point in trying to change her situation, so "helpless" is the best answer.

8. The correct answer is C. The word "resigned" is a synonym of the phrase "mute and hopeless" in the last sentence.

9. The correct answer is A. The second sentence of the last paragraph mentions that power stations "have been the culprit of the bulk of the acid in rainwater in recent years," meaning that they are the largest contributor to the problem.

10. The correct answer is D. Paragraph 1 is devoted exclusively to the topic of eye shadow, while paragraph 2 talks about eye liner, lip and cheek color, nail polish, and hair dye, so the best summaries are "Ancient Egyptian eye shadow" for the first paragraph and "Other ancient cosmetics" for the second paragraph.

11. The correct answer is D. The passage provides information for most fully the question: "What is the background to and definition of the term 'liberal arts education'?" The other questions relate only to specific points from the passage, instead of the entire passage.

12. The correct answer is C. The primary purpose of the passage is to provide background information about Beethoven's life and work. The passage begins by providing information about the composer's musical training, before going on to talk about his professional life and compositions.

13. The correct answer is B. The passage uses the phrases "people . . . die needlessly" and "fresh water saves lives." Therefore, it is the writer's

viewpoint that the deaths could be avoided. The information in answers A, C, and D is not stated in the passage.

14. The correct answer is D. The passage uses the word "prescience," which means insight, to describe Newton in the topic sentence. Later, the writer uses the phrases "because of Newton's work . . . we currently understand" and "As a result of Newton's investigation . . . we know today." Therefore, the writer believes that Newton made a significant achievement.

15. The correct answer is A. The passage states that "computer-to-computer trading could result in a downturn in the stock market." Further, this downturn could result in a "computer-led stock market crash." In order to avoid these negative results, the regulations are needed. Answers B and C are not stated in the passage. Answer D is incorrect because the passage talks about how the use of computers has changed over time.

16. The correct answer is B. When explaining the idea of assimilation, the passage uses the phrase "are examples of" to show that breast and bottle feeding are being used as examples. Note that "exemplify" means to give an example.

17. The correct answer is D. The author implies that a radioactive leak would have dire consequences since he opens the passage with this sentence: "Highly concentrated radioactive waste is lethal and can remain so for thousands of years."

18. The correct answer is A. The author mentions Angelou's childhood abuse most likely in order to give an example of the hardship that she faced. After mentioning the examples from Angelou's life, the passage explains that "Her writings are widely regarded as celebrating the African-American experience, as well as the capacity [. . .] to survive hardship."

19. The correct answer is A. "Mitigating" means to lessen the seriousness of something.

20. The correct answer is C. "Nebulous" means unclear or without structure.

Made in the USA
Middletown, DE
15 March 2022

62722650R00064